MAKE YOUR OWN DAMN CHEESE

John A. Chuback, MD

Health Communications, Inc.
Deerfield Beach, Florida

www.hcibooks.com

**Library of Congress Cataloging-in-Publication Data
is available through the Library of Congress**

ISBN-13: 978-07573-2182-5 (Paperback)
ISBN-10: 07573-2182-8 (Paperback)
ISBN-13: 978-07573-2183-2 (ePub)
ISBN-10: 07573-2183-6 (ePub)

Publisher: Health Communications, Inc.
   3201 S.W. 15th Street
   Deerfield Beach, FL 33442–8190

Cover and interior design by Lawna Patterson Oldfield
Interior illustrations by Larissa Hise Henoch

Contents

It is out of profound respect that I dedicate this book
to Jim Rohn, Bob Proctor, Brian Tracy, Denis Waitley,
Price Pritchett, Earl Nightingale, and Napoleon Hill for the
incredible contributions they have made to
the field of personal development.
Each of these men has demonstrated an extraordinary
passion for teaching and sharing through their work.
Their efforts to educate those who are serious about self-improvement
have been extraordinary, both individually and collectively.
They have helped enormously in bringing to the "common person"
an awareness of the immense potential of the human mind.
The positive impact they have had on millions of people over
the years and around the world is truly immeasurable.

For anyone who is interested in becoming the best
they can be, I strongly suggest you study the books, recordings,
programs, and seminars offered by each of these teachers.
Doing so will be an investment in yourself, which will
pay dividends for as long as you live.

Special Thanks to:

James Allen

Andrew Carnegie

John Paul DeJoria

Walt Disney

Thomas Edison

Ralph Waldo Emerson

Chuck Feeney

Henry Ford

Viktor Frankl

Milton Friedman

Brian Greene

Sir Edmund Hillary

William James

Spencer Johnson

Deepak Malhotra

Dick Portillo

Ayn Rand

David J. Schwartz

Thomas Sowell

W. Clement Stone

Henry David Thoreau

Sam Walton

Orville Wright

Wilbur Wright

"We live today in a golden age.
This is an era that man has looked
forward to, dreamed of, and worked toward
for thousands of years. But since it's here,
we pretty well take it for granted.
We in America are particularly fortunate
to live in the richest land that ever
existed on the face of the Earth.
A land of abundant opportunity
for everyone."

—Earl Nightingale
The Strangest Secret, 1957

Chapter 1

Earl Loved to Read

Once upon a time, in a maze not so far away, there lived a young mouse named Earl. He was a very curious mouse and wondered ceaselessly about the little maze he was born into. He yearned for a better life. He wanted more than the maze had to offer. Earl loved to read and felt fortunate to have found two wonderful books about mice, and "little people," and their relationship with cheese and the maze they lived in. The books were widely believed to contain great wisdom and insight into how to live a good life.

The first little book seemed to say that there was an invisible outside source that provided all the cheese in the maze. These mysterious outsiders appeared to control where the cheese would appear in the maze, when it would appear, and how much cheese would materialize when it did. This book taught that a smart mouse should have the courage to leave his current cheese station to explore the maze if and when it appeared that the cheese supply was coming to an end. This seemed very logical. Every smart mouse Earl knew saw this as very wise advice.

Then Earl read the second little book and became confused. This book seemed to say that everyone was mistaken. They had been living under the spell of a powerful illusion. According to book number two, the mice did not live within a physical maze. The startling revelation was that, in fact, the maze was *in the mouse*. It also appeared to Earl that the second little book was suggesting that in order to be "a mouse like no other" one should escape the maze by whatever means one could.

After thinking long and hard about the two books, Earl decided he wouldn't stand for a lifetime of pursuing cheese without the possibility of finding happiness. He made up his mind to become "a mouse like no other" and get out of the maze, even though no one had ever *really* explained what was outside. From his reading, he deduced that whatever there was out there must be better than what the maze had to offer.

Earl didn't have the strength to crash through a wall, nor a friend powerful enough to throw him on top of the maze. He certainly didn't have the magical ability to walk through walls as if they didn't exist; so, Earl thought seriously about how a mouse like himself could actually get out. After lots of thinking, he decided to *dig* his way out! He was fortunate to find a pick-axe and a shovel in a remote, rarely travelled, area of the maze. He began immediately to tunnel his way outside of the physical maze that imprisoned him.

Earl was able to chop through the floor of the maze without much effort and found himself in the earth beneath it. Once there, he began to burrow laterally in one direction. Earl created a long underground passageway, and when he felt he'd gone a far enough distance, he began picking up above his head, expecting to find freedom outside the maze. To his dismay, as he surfaced, he found what looked like the underside of the maze. "No problem," Earl thought to himself, "I'll just dig a little farther to the side and try again. This little maze of mine must be bigger than I thought."

Days went by, and then months, but Earl had no luck in getting beyond the limits of the maze. He did everything he could to figure out a path to liberation, but no matter which direction he had dug, and no matter how long a tunnel he created, he always came up against the floor of the maze.

Ultimately, he was so desperate to be free, he wondered if what appeared to be the floor of the maze was actually the floor of the world outside of the maze and managed to pick-axe his way through. Sadly, again and again, he always found himself inside the same maze he was trying to escape. At the end of each day of relentless digging, he had to eventually resign himself to crawling back out of the tunnel the same way he got in, finding himself right where he started . . . inside the maze.

Earl was so committed to this approach to self-emancipation that he probably would have died in this endeavor, either from exhaustion or old age. Fortunately, that's when Earl met Napoleon.

Chapter 2

I'm Napoleon

One evening, after a long day of strenuous tunneling that once again lead nowhere, Earl emerged back into the maze, tired, covered in dirt, and famished. But this night was a night like no other. This night was different, because on this night an elderly mouse with thinning grey hair and wire-rimmed glasses was sitting quietly next to the hole in the floor when Earl emerged. Earl was a bit startled to find another mouse in his corner of the maze. He brushed himself off, hoping to look a bit more presentable in front of his unexpected visitor.

The elderly mouse introduced himself quietly and confidently with the simple statement, "I'm Napoleon."

At first, Earl had to fight back the urge to chuckle; and say, "Nice to make your acquaintance. I'm Cyrus the Great." Fortunately, he was able to resist the temptation to be humorous and after a brief pause he responded, "Pleased to meet you, Napoleon, my name is Earl." At that moment, there was no way for Earl to know that this unexpected encounter would change his life forever.

Chapter 3

A New Direction

"**M**ay I ask you a question, Earl?" Napoleon queried.

"Of course," said the younger mouse.

"What were you doing down in that hole?"

"I was trying to get out. I was trying to escape from the maze," Earl replied.

"I see," said Napoleon. "Why would you want to do that?"

"To find freedom," Earl responded confidently. "To find freedom and happiness, and to forget about cheese."

"Are you unhappy?" asked Napoleon with concern in his voice.

"Well," said Earl, "I'm not sure how to describe the way I feel. I do know one thing, though; I'm definitely *not satisfied* with life in this maze. I feel like there's no chance of living a good life in here. I think that if I could just get out of here, everything would be better."

"Really?" asked Napoleon. "Where did you get the idea that a panacea exists outside the maze? I'd like you to consider one thing, Earl. Consider that happiness and satisfaction are *not* the same thing. You should always be happy, but never satisfied. Dissatisfaction is a creative state. As long as you are somewhat dissatisfied with one aspect or another of your life, you will always be motivated to make it better. The key is to remain happy throughout that process. It's a wonderful process, once you fully understand it and embrace it. If we were always satisfied, there would be no incentive for us to do what is necessary to improve ourselves. There would be no reason to grow.

"I can see your point, Napoleon, but I've read books,"

said Earl. "I have been enlightened. I now understand that the 'mice who are like no others' don't really need much cheese, if they need any cheese at all. I have also learned that I can be free—if only I could get out of this stupid maze. If I decide to stay inside the maze, the best I can do is to accept that change is inevitable and spend my life chasing the cheese. I don't want to waste the rest of my days trying to anticipate where the people in control will move the cheese next, or how much cheese they will decide to leave for me."

"Earl," began Napoleon, "did these books explain, how a mouse survives without cheese, what cheese is, or what is outside the maze that is so wonderful?"

"Not really," said Earl, "but it seemed that a clever mouse was either very skillful at chasing and finding the big piles of cheese or escaping the maze and being done with their need for cheese.

"I also learned that there is a maze inside of me. I learned that it's this 'inner maze' that really holds me captive. So, I figured if I could dig my way out of the big maze, I'd be free of the little maze inside me, too. You see, I just want to be happy and free. That's all I really want."

"Fascinating," said Napoleon. "Earl," he continued, "if you don't mind very much, I'd like to take you away from your digging for a little while to introduce you to a very important mouse. I think it may help you find what you're looking for without so much back-breaking work. I think this experience will help point you in a better direction. I hope you don't take this the wrong way, but downward doesn't seem to be working too well for you. Would that be okay with you? Would you like to meet this mouse if I could arrange an introduction?"

"Well, I could use some rest, I suppose," answered Earl wearily. "And I do enjoy meeting new mice, especially when they can help me find my way to where I'd like to go. Sure, Napoleon, I'd be happy to meet this mouse; but, who is it?"

Napoleon smiled as a twinkle of excitement flashed in his eyes. "It's you, Earl. The mouse I'd like you to meet is *you*."

Chapter 4

The Four Teachers

"**M**e?" asked Earl in astonishment. "How can I meet me? I already *know* me. Is this some kind of joke or game?"

"No Earl," answered Napoleon solemnly. "This is neither a joke nor a game. I know how serious you are about living the best life you can and enjoying a wonderful future. I wouldn't waste your time with trifles and nonsense. I believe you still have much to learn about yourself and the maze you live in.

"You see," Earl, I feel that each of the books you read were partly right, but certainly not completely right. The truth of the matter is that the mouse *is* inside a maze, just like the first book says. The maze we live in not only exists, but it is absolutely inescapable. There is nothing beyond the maze. The maze is infinite; it's boundless. There are no edges to the maze. There is no top to the maze and there is no bottom to the maze. The maze is our universe. The maze we live in is called *reality*.

In addition, it's also true that there *is* a maze inside the mouse, just like the second book says. But, no mouse can *ever* expel the inner maze. Every mouse has a maze inside of him or her. Those are called *the facts*. That being said, all of these truths are just fine. This is simply the way things are. There is no reason to worry or to be afraid. In fact, if you understand the maze you live in, and you understand the maze that lives inside of you, then you and *you alone* can make all of your dreams come true."

"Wow," said Earl sounding scared and excited all at the same time, "now, I'm totally confused."

"Don't fret youngster," said Napoleon. "I have some

friends who will help me explain how things work. Once they have had a chance to educate you as to the way things really are, you will see it all very clearly."

Earl didn't really believe what Napoleon was saying at this point, but he believed that Napoleon believed it. And, for some reason, that was good enough for Earl.

Napoleon then went on to tell Earl that he was going to introduce him to four great teachers. Their names were Bob, Brian, Denis, and Jim. They were wise old mice who had spent a lifetime studying how mice think, feel, and behave. These mice not only understood the inner and outer maze but were also gifted in their ability to share these insights with others. Earl was eager to meet these brilliant educators. Earl and Napoleon agreed to convene early the next morning and set off on their quest deep into the heart of the maze where the four teachers could be found.

Chapter 5

The Mind Mouse

As promised, Napoleon appeared just past dawn and found Earl eagerly waiting and ready to go. The journey was long, but Napoleon knew the path well. They steadily traversed the winding labyrinth to a place far deeper in the maze than Earl had ever been. In fact, Earl was shocked by the immensity of the maze. His little section of the maze seemed so small and so limited by comparison.

After a half-day walk, they finally arrived at their destination. Seated comfortably in a group, they found the four teachers quietly awaiting them.

"Gentlemen," Napoleon announced, "this is Earl."

Each mouse gestured in polite salutation.

"I believe he is going to be a very gifted student." Napoleon went on. "He loves to learn. He has been studying books, but I'm not sure he understands everything he knows. I found him trying to dig his way out of the maze by creating a tunnel. It seems his reading inspired him to do so. It also seems, based on his reading, that he has had his fill of cheese. He was looking to escape the maze. He was hoping to have what's outside the maze instead."

"Outside the maze?" Jim started immediately. "There is nothing outside the maze. The maze goes on forever. It has no beginning and no end. So, I think we can agree to leave that enterprise behind us, yes?"

"Yes," began Earl, "if you're sure."

"I'm quite sure!" interrupted the mouse with wispy white hair, his reading glasses positioned precariously near the end of his nose. "I'm absolutely certain there is nothing beyond the maze. The maze is the real world. You cannot conquer the maze by trying to run away from it or by making believe that it doesn't exist."

"Yes, Sir," said Earl in a respectful and sincere tone of voice. "I understand. That makes perfect sense to me."

Napoleon spoke again. "I think young Earl here has been convinced that it would serve him well to purge his inner maze. I think he believes he would be liberated somehow if he could eliminate the maze that lives within him. He has come to understand the inner maze the same way he sees the outer maze, like a prison of some kind."

Now it was Bob's turn to speak. Bob was a tall, slim, impeccably dressed mouse with a full head of perfectly coiffed white hair. "Earl, this may sound like a strange question, but have you ever seen your mind?"

My mind? My mind! Have I ever seen my mind? I think this guy may be cracked! I think he may have a screw loose, Earl thought to himself. But, rather than expressing his incredulity, he said, "No. I have never seen my mind. How could I have seen my mind?"

"You couldn't, Earl," said Bob. "That's the whole point. We are visual creatures. We understand through seeing images in the mind's eye. If you don't have an image of your mind to work with, it's almost impossible to truly understand how your mind works or how to work with your mind to create the life you so greatly desire."

"Extraordinary," said Earl. "But what am I to do since I can't see my mind?"

"Excellent question," responded Bob, his voice filled with excitement. "I'm going to show you how it looks! I'm going to introduce you to the 'mind mouse.' It may be the most powerful thing you'll ever learn."

And with that, Bob produced a piece of black chalk and began to draw on the white wall of the maze. "Let this large circle represent your head," he began as he drew a large circle on the wall. "And let this represent your body," he said as he continued to sketch a rudimentary figure of a mouse. What Bob created looked just like this:

Then he created two horizontal lines, equally spaced from one side of the head to the other and said, "Your mind is divided into three mental zones. In the middle you have the *conscious mind*. Beneath that, separated by the psychic barrier, is the *subconscious mind*, and at the very top is the *superconscious mind*. Remember," he said, "this is not the anatomy of your *brain*, this is a schematic representation of your *mind*. There's a very big difference." What he drew now looked like this:

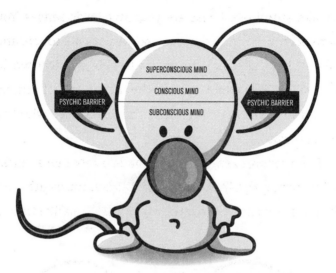

"Earl," Bob continued, "this is the basic structure of your mind. Seeing it will help you immensely in understanding it. And, understanding it will change you, and your life, forever. Now, let's talk about how it works.

"Let's begin with the central zone. Again, this represents the conscious mind. Your conscious mind is your thinking mind. This is your intellectual and academic mind. There are five sensory inputs into the conscious mind through which the conscious mind connects with, and is exposed to, the outside world. These five inputs are like antennae. These are your five basic senses. You were born with the ability to see, hear, taste, touch, and smell. These senses connect us to the physical world we live in. They connect us to the maze. And, of critical importance, they connect us to the other mice who live in the maze."

Bob turned to the wall and made a few more marks representing the five antennae that communicate with the conscious mind. Now the drawing looked like this:

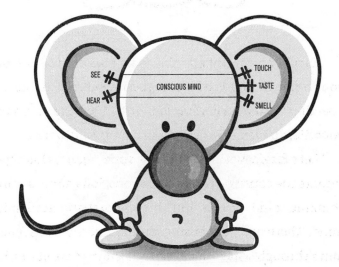

At this point Brian, another white-haired mouse, pro-fessionally outfitted in a handsome suit and tie, inter-jected a very important statement. "Earl," he said seriously but energetically, "the conscious mind is very important. It's important because it is the thinking mind; and that is of critical importance because you will become what you think about most of the time. *Never* forget those words. They are perhaps the most important words you'll ever hear. Again, these are the six essential words to remember: *you become what you think about,*" he repeated slowly and clearly, gesturing with his hands to put emphasis on the importance of the phrase.

Jim jumped in, "I suggest you adopt that little phrase as a cornerstone of your *personal philosophy*, Earl. If you take the time to really look at the maze you live in, you will be able to see *exactly* what you have been thinking about most of the time. That's very important to understand."

Earl was listening intently. He was totally engaged. He had never heard anything like this before. He was curious where this would all lead. He was beginning to wonder if any of the mice he had met before had any idea what they were talking about. He was quickly becoming convinced that the mice he grew up around back in his section of the maze knew nothing at all. He was astonished. He was also filled with excitement and enthusiasm. He was ready to learn more.

Bob continued, "Let me explain this a little more deeply for you, Earl. You see, what the conscious mind predominantly thinks about, and focuses on, will eventually cross the psychic barrier into the subconscious mind. The subconscious mind is also called the *emotional mind*. This is where the 'inner maze' you read about resides. The inner maze exists in your subconscious mind. We have a term for this maze that lives inside of you. We call it *the paradigm.*"

"Paradigm?" repeated Earl with an air of confusion in his voice, indicating that he had never heard this word before.

"Yes, Earl . . . paradigm," Bob responded.

"What's a paradigm?" asked Earl.

"Excellent question," said Bob. "A paradigm is a group of habits that will predominantly drive your actions and determine the results you achieve in the physical maze you live in. The paradigm almost exclusively determines how you behave and interact with the world around you. These habits will greatly define how much cheese you will enjoy. Ultimately, your results are action driven and your actions are driven by your paradigm. Here, let me show you how it looks using the mind mouse figure." Bob made a few additional notations and stepped back so that Earl could see this:

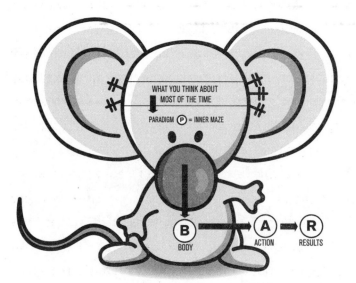

"What's most interesting," said Bob, "is that it's *primarily* the mice that surround us, and the mice with whom we choose to scurry around, that influence what we think about most of the time. It's predominantly what we hear and see that determine our most frequent thoughts. These thoughts will also be affected by the books we read, the foods we eat, the television programs we watch, the radio stations we tune into, the places we go, the news we take in, and the overall experiences we live through. We can represent these predominant thoughts with an X. Let X represent what you think about most of the time. With enough time, because you focus mostly on them, this X group of thoughts will percolate through the psychic barrier and you will become emotionally involved with them. They will eventually take root in your subconscious mind.

"The subconscious mind doesn't have the ability to reject. It's like a flower bed containing nutrient rich, perfectly fertile soil. Whatever idea 'seeds' you plant there will grow vigorously, and with deep roots. The subconscious mind doesn't care what 'seeds' you plant. It has no biases, inclinations, or preferences. It cannot discern good ideas from bad ideas, positive thoughts from negative thoughts, or truth from fiction. The garden simply reflects the thoughts planted by the conscious mind. It has no choice but to germinate the seeds that *you* sow.

"Your conscious mind will, over time, program your paradigm to be in harmony with the things you think about most of the time. Thus, you will have adopted an *X paradigm*. The X paradigm will in turn define a collection of habits that are expressed as *X actions* and give *X results*. Let me show you:

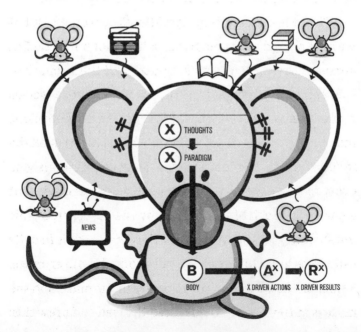

"Do you see it?" asked Bob, knowing he had given Earl a lot to consider in a very short period of time.

"Yes, Bob," said Earl in a steady voice. "I must admit, I have never seen anything like this before in my entire life, but I get it. I think I truly understand."

"That's good," interjected Denis, a red-haired mouse with kind eyes and a pleasant smile. Until now, he had been quietly listening to all that had been said. "That's good, because there is much more to the big picture.

"Please listen carefully, Earl." Denis continued. "What we have shared with you to this point is not only true, but also very powerful. You must understand the strength of the relationship between the conscious and subconscious mind. The conscious mind will direct the subconscious mind to develop the paradigm, which you have called the inner maze. Every mouse thinks almost continuously, so every mouse develops a paradigm. None of us is without a paradigm. Each of us is driven by the blueprint of this inner maze. And the structure of the inner maze is *heavily* influenced by the input we get from the outer maze. Remember," said Denis, "the mouse *is* in the maze, and the maze *is* in the mouse." Denis faced the wall and drew this:

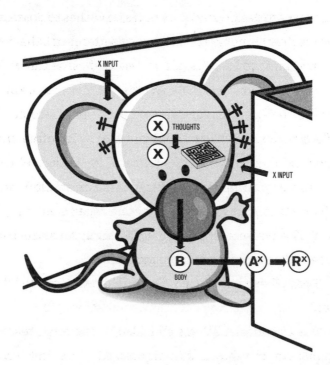

"Our environment largely determines what we think about and, in the end, how we behave. The interplay between our thinking and our actions we call the *psychosomatic* relationship. *Psycho* (the mind) controls *soma* (the body). Unless a mouse is very careful about his thinking, he can become a victim of this relationship. But, if a mouse is clever, he can use his knowledge of how this works to design any inner maze he wishes to possess. The resultant inner maze will dictate patterns of behavior and preconceived results. If a mouse wishes, he can willfully and deliberately create an outer maze fit for a king. You see, the key is to make sure that the maze becomes a reflection of what the mouse *really* wants. Too often, the mouse becomes a reflection of a maze he dislikes. When you master your understanding of this information, you will find that you are in control of 'the experiment' in the maze. The mouse will no longer be learning the maze. The maze will now be learning the mouse."

"Really?" exclaimed Earl. "Quick! Tell me! How do I do that?"

"Easy, youngster," Denis chuckled, as the other teachers and Napoleon smiled in amusement. "We first have to be certain that you truly understand the power and seriousness of the relationship between your thoughts, the paradigm, and your results."

Seriousness? What could be so serious about living like a king? Earl thought to himself.

"Okay, Denis, what is it I must understand?" he asked, still sounding a bit impatient.

"Well son, you must understand that you have to *master* this material, so that you remain in control of the paradigm. You must be in command of your thinking mind so that it is focused on only those good things you want in the maze. You will be the architect of the maze you live in, good or bad. If you allow your mind to be filled with negative, self-defeating, fearful thoughts, you will attract failure and disappointment. Your paradigm will reflect the negativity of your conscious mind, and so will your actions. In the end, you will always live in the maze you have been trying to escape because negativity and fear dominated your thinking. I like to recite a little poem about the subconscious mind and the inner maze it holds. It goes like this:

> I have a little mouse-robot that goes around with me
> I tell him what I'm thinking, I tell him what I see,
> I tell my little mouse-robot all my hopes and fears,
> It listens and remembers everything it hears
>
> At first my little mouse-robot followed my command,
> But after years of training, it's gotten out of hand

It doesn't care what's right or wrong,
Nor what is false or true

No matter what I try now,
It tells me what to do!"

"I think I understand," said Earl. "You're saying that if I'm not careful, I will create a terrible inner maze by thinking constantly about what I *don't* want and what I *don't* like. The resulting paradigm will drive me to build an outer maze that's fit for a pauper instead of a king. Is that correct?"

"You've got it, Earl. Napoleon was right. You're a very good student," said Denis.

"Thank you, Sir. I'm eager to learn, because I'm not satisfied with my current life here in the maze."

"The maze you live in is a reflection of how you've been thinking, Earl. I think it's time we construct a new maze for you. That starts with making sure that there is a beautiful, successful, happy maze inside of you. Everything depends on what is planted in your emotional mind."

"That's what worries me," responded Earl despondently. "I'm afraid my paradigmatic maze, the one I've programmed for myself over all these years, is a terrible place. It's a blueprint for mediocrity, failure, and unhappiness."

"You're exactly right, Earl. That does describe your paradigm, and it's reflected by the unfulfilling life you live in the maze. That's precisely why you wanted to run away. That's the bad news. The good news is, you can tear down that maze and replace it with a brand-new maze. You can build the maze of your dreams," said Jim, looking Earl square in the eye.

"But how?" asked Earl. "How can I reprogram my paradigm and design a better maze? I'm sick and tired of this old mouse trap I've been caught in for all these years."

"Well said!" exclaimed Bob. "I like that. Very good, Earl! You *are* a bright lad, aren't you? Well look," he said, "let's go back to our drawing for a moment and see what we can do about your present state of mind and circumstances.

"Let's see what happens if we change what you think about most of the time. Let's call this new way of thinking the Y *idea*."

Bob turned back to the wall of the maze and replaced the X in the conscious mind with a Y, like so:

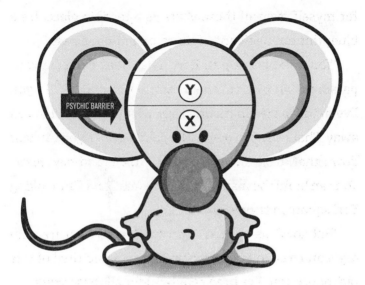

"I see it!" said Earl bursting with excitement. "So, all I need to do is think the successful, happy, prosperous thoughts I so desire, and I'll change the maze that lives within me! Right? And then, the maze I live within will automatically transform itself to reflect the maze I carry around with me in my emotional mind! I mean that's right, isn't it? I know that's how it works!"

Earl was so elated he couldn't contain himself. He was exuberant. All of his problems were solved. All of his prayers and hopes and dreams had been answered. It was so clear. It was so easy! This was the greatest day of his life.

"Not so fast," said Bob, bringing Earl back down to earth with a thud. "You're absolutely correct that that is, in general, the way it works. The problem is, it's *far* from easy. In fact, it is very, very hard.

"Look Earl, there is another barrier we need to make you aware of. Just as there is a psychic barrier separating the conscious mind from the subconscious mind, there is also something called the *terror barrier* that separates the maze *you* live in from a much better maze, which exists in a parallel realm. Because of how you've been thinking, you've never been able to see or experience the parallel maze."

Wait. What? Earl thought to himself. *Terror barrier? Parallel maze? What planet are these guys from?* he wondered. Just when he was starting to get it, he began to question once again if he was surrounded by a bunch of nuts.

"We're not nuts if that's what you're wondering," said Brian, who had been quiet for some time. We know exactly what we're talking about. Stick with it and trust us. It gets a little more difficult from here on out, but you're a very intelligent mouse. It will all come together if you pay close attention and have faith."

"That's right," Bob continued. "You see, the paradigm despises change. As you attempt to introduce the Y idea, the paradigm will immediately kick it out of the subconscious mind before it can take root. The emotional mind will maintain the previously accepted X idea as the paradigm for as long as it possibly can. That's just the nature of the subconscious mind. When you hold an idea in your *heart*, another name for the subconscious mind, you are emotionally involved with it. The idea becomes a group of habits and the subconscious mind falls in love with them. Changing the paradigm is like trying to break up a great romance. Every mouse becomes totally at ease with his paradigm. No matter how poorly designed the paradigm, it becomes comfortable to the mouse because it's so familiar. It's like a dysfunctional relationship; bad for those involved, but difficult to dissolve.

"You would think the subconscious mind would be eager to take on a better collection of habits; but it's not. It will fight like hell to keep things just the way they are. The body is always working to maintain homeostasis, a steady state. It has evolved over eons to maintain an unwavering core temperature, a blood pressure in a very narrow range, a stable heart rhythm, and a stable heart rate. It also works feverishly to maintain its current paradigm. The body sees any change or instability as a potentially life-threatening danger.

"Introducing a Y idea puts the physical body of the mouse into a negative vibration . . . a state of unbearable 'dis-ease.' In order to avert such intolerable feelings, the mouse quickly reverts to X thinking and X actions, which are congruous with the paradigm. With the new idea successfully defeated, he feels comfortable again. Ironically, he feels better even though the old way of thinking yields the same X results he wished to alter and improve. Change is uncomfortable. It can even be painful.

"Think of how mice you know react when they try to quit smoking, start a new career, or lose weight, for example. It's never easy, and very often results in failure. There is a sort of peace, albeit pathological, which one finds in the status quo. Remarkably, the average mouse trying to shed a few ounces typically prefers the negative

emotions associated with remaining overweight and stay-
ing in their personal *comfort zone*, to the unpleasant
feelings associated with introducing a new nutritional
program or exercise routine.

"Look at these drawings and see if they make sense to
you at this point," Bob said as he turned once again to
make two new images of the mind mouse, one above the
other:

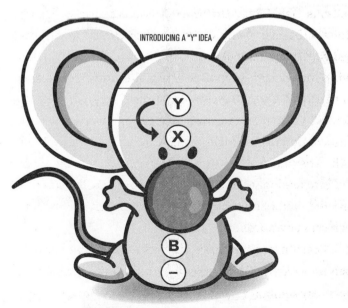

When a "Y" idea is introduced to the subconscious mind, the body
goes into a negative vibration and a state of "dis-ease."

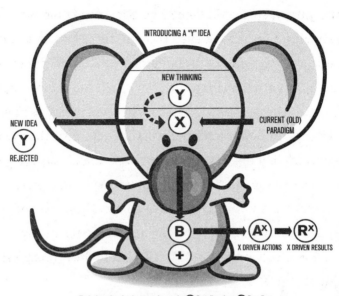

Typical results of trying to exchange the (X) Paradigm for a (Y) Paradigm.
The (Y) idea is most often quickly rejected. Body returns to a positive vibration and the
comfort zone. Unfortunately, the results remain the same as they reflect the old paradigm (X).

"Yes, they do make sense to me," said Earl, after taking a fair amount of time to really consider what the drawings were depicting.

"You know," he said sincerely, "I have felt that way before; I just never understood what I was experiencing when it was happening. When I try to change, I become uncomfortable. I don't feel well. I get very uneasy, anxious, and jittery; so, I quit. Once I go back to my old way of behaving, I feel better, even though the results have not improved. My life is still the same. I'm disappointed and unhappy with the old results, but it still feels better than the disturbing emotions I experience when I try to make a change. And, you're right. Sometimes it's more than just emotions. My body is affected as well: I don't sleep; I get headaches; my stomach gets upset; I become a physical wreck. But it's interesting—as soon as I give up and go back to my old ways, I start feeling better right away."

"Excellent," said Brian. "You're making the connections. That's fantastic.

"Now," Brian continued, "let's go a little further, Earl. I think you're going to like this part. Let's talk about what I like to call the *superconscious mind*."

"This is so cool," said Bob. A warm smile shimmered in Denis's eyes as they narrowed just a bit. Jim gently tapped the piece of chalk he was holding against the floor of the maze. He whistled quietly as if to say, "Whoa, this is some heavy stuff we're about to get into." The stage was set to move forward in understanding the mind of a mouse even more completely.

Bob tossed the chalk he was holding to Brian and said, "Take it away, old friend."

Brian snatched the chalk out of the air with cat-like reflexes and began to draw. He created a vertical line connecting the subconscious and the superconscious mind as follows:

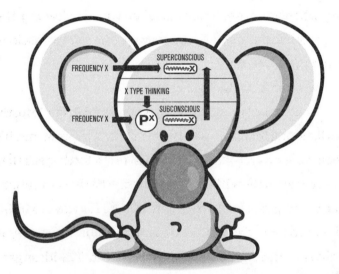

The frequency of the subconscious mind reflects the paradigm. This determines the frequency of the superconscious mind. They will be in harmony with each other.

"Look at this, Earl," Brian started. "Just as the conscious mind programs the paradigm in the subconscious mind, the subconscious mind then shares the paradigmatic frequency it has been tuned to with the superconscious mind. The superconscious mind is always active no matter what else is going on. Whether you know it or not, the superconscious mind is always functioning. When you are actively thinking with the conscious mind, when you are working, when you are talking, when you are listening, when you are eating, *even when you are sleeping*, the superconscious mind is functioning. The superconscious mind never rests."

"What is it doing?" asked Earl.

"That's another excellent question," said Brian. "Mostly it's listening for and working on solutions to problems. It's looking for novel answers that will bring forth ideas that are in harmony with the paradigm. It strives to satisfy the paradigm. It is constantly searching for ways to fulfill the needs and desires of the paradigm and ultimately it delivers these ideas to the conscious mind. The ideas generated by the superconscious mind seem to appear out of thin air. They often 'flash' onto the screen of the *mind's eye* out of nowhere."

"The mind's eye?" asked Earl curiously. "I remember hearing that term earlier."

"Yes, the mind's eye," responded Bob. "Again, we are visual creatures. We think in pictures. When we daydream or think or use our creative imagination, we see vivid images in what is sometimes called the 'third eye.' It tends to be located in the center of the forehead. This is where we see this spectacular picture show.

"Often, these ideas come to us from the superconscious mind, not in bits and pieces but, rather, in a complete form. Sometimes the idea may look like a single-frame snapshot, but at other times it's like seeing a two-hour movie from beginning to end in a single moment. It's quite extraordinary. The superconscious mind often reveals these images when we least expect them. The superconscious mind works like an egg incubator, warming and nurturing the ideas that we have attracted through the *universal intelligence*.

"No one knows the 'gestational period' for each of these new ideas, but the moment they mature, the superconscious mind acts like a film projector, casting the image onto the mind's eye in full technicolor and high definition. This can happen during sleep or when we're wide awake. *Boom!* Just like that! Without even thinking about what may be troubling you, or what it is that you want to achieve, like a lightning bolt, there it is in all its glory—the solution. The answer you've been looking for. It's literally phenomenal.

"Look," said Brian as he finished another sketch, "you can think of it like this:"

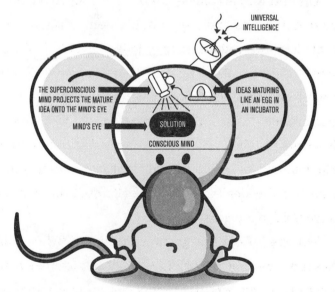

"I see it," said Earl. "But how does it work? That doesn't seem to make any sense at all! How can the superconscious be working all the time and finding answers without us even consciously thinking about it? How does it just pull ideas, answers, and solutions out of thin air like that?" demanded Earl.

"You've arrived at a very important point," said Brian. "You don't have to understand *how* it works. You just have to understand that it *does* work."

"Okay," said Earl. "I'll accept that. But, just to be sure I've got this straight, I'm still in control, right? I mean, once I begin to apply what you're all teaching me. My conscious mind sees in pictures what I want and how I want to live. That, in turn, programs my subconscious mind to set the paradigm to the frequency I desire. Then, the subconscious mind tunes the superconscious mind to the same frequency so that it can begin listening for answers, yes?"

"That's it!" said Brian. "You've got it exactly! And the superconscious mind will assist in the process by accessing the invisible powers of the universal intelligence."

"Great!" shouted Earl. "So, we're done, right?"

"Wrong!" exclaimed Napoleon and the four teachers in unison.

"Wrong?" squealed Earl, sounding annoyed. "I want to go back to my corner of the maze and quit!"

Brian laughed and said cheerfully, "Don't quit on us yet. Don't let your old paradigm get the best of you, Earl. We're getting there. Don't get impatient."

"Okay," said Earl, "I won't quit. I'm committed to the journey."

"Now," began Brian, "look here," he said as he started once again to draw on the wall. "The superconscious mind has what's equivalent to a satellite dish listening to the universe for waves of energy that are in harmony with the paradigm. You will only be able to hear vibrations and receive signals from transmitting sources that are in absolute harmony with your paradigm. These are the *unseen forces* and *phantom powers* that you can't see or touch; but they are definitely there.

"These *invisible waves* emanate from what we call the *universal intelligence*, which is comprised of *infinite knowledge*. The infinite knowledge is all the knowledge that has ever existed or will ever exist. This body of knowledge is present in all places at all times. The superconscious mind is always in search of the energy you are

pursuing. And, this is very important to understand—
that same energy is searching for you. You won't attract—
can't attract in fact—anything that isn't in tune with the
maze that lives inside the mouse. The paradigm sets the
bandwidth to which your superconscious mind is tuned."
Brian stepped away so that Earl could see:

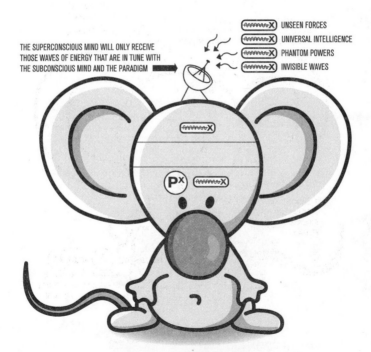

The frequency of the subconscious mind reflects the paradigm. This determines the
frequency of the superconscious mind. They will be in harmony with each other.

Brian sat down and handed the chalk to Bob, who was already walking briskly toward the blackboard, eager to continue. "Check this out," he said as he drew what looked like a broadcasting tower coming off of the subconscious mind on the mind mouse. It looked like this:

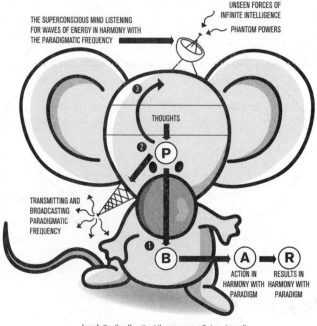

Law of attraction: You attract the same energy that you transmit.
The frequency of this energy is dictated by the paradigm.

"So, let's recap briefly," Bob said. "What you think about most of the time in the conscious mind will eventually cross the psychic barrier and take hold in the subconscious mind. This will define your personal paradigm. This is the maze that is in every mouse. It determines what 'station' your 'heart' will be tuned to. The paradigm will, in turn, be manifest as a collection of habits. The psychosomatic connection that exists in each of us will dictate how your body will act and behave. The paradigm will almost exclusively determine what results you achieve as a consequence of your behavior. In other words, your body 'dances' to the music of the station you've tuned your paradigm to. Second, the paradigm tunes the superconscious mind to the same frequency so that it only listens for energy in harmony with the paradigm. And third . . ."

"Third!" Earl screamed. "Third? What is this? You must be kidding!"

"Yes, third, and last, if that makes you feel any better," said Bob as Napoleon, Jim, Denis, and Brian roared with laughter, "third, the subconscious mind continuously broadcasts the same paradigmatic frequency out to the universe."

Jim whistled quietly again. It was one long, low note, barely audible. This was definitely another "whoa, that's deep" moment.

"So, we are giving off vibrations?" asked Earl.

"All the time," said Bob. "You're giving off vibrations as waves of energy. You're broadcasting them out around the world and deep into space. You're much more powerful than you've been lead to believe. Just as you can see the rays of light being produced by the sun millions of miles away, you are shining your energy waves right back upon it. That's the way it works, believe it or not."

"Fascinating," said Earl.

"Very," said Napoleon.

Chapter 6

Cheese

At this point, just as Earl was beginning to get the hang of this new way of looking at himself and the world around him, it was time to take all of this understanding to the next level. It was certainly interesting enough to see how the mind of a mouse worked, but what was the practical application of all this? How could this change a mouse's life?

"So," Jim began, "you'd like to live *the good life*; is that right, Earl?"

"That's correct, Sir," Earl answered with renewed excitement.

"The good life is expensive. It takes a lot of cheese." Bob interjected. "There's another way to live that doesn't cost as much, but it isn't any good."

"So true," Denis chimed in.

"That's a very good point," Jim agreed. "Let's talk about cheese for a moment. Cheese is a very important subject. Did the other two books tell you about cheese, Earl?"

"Well, they certainly talked a lot about cheese. They seemed to imply that most mice are preoccupied with cheese. They often spend their lives chasing cheese and oftentimes they never find happiness, no matter how much cheese they get. Then again, it seems mice who find themselves without much cheese also seem unhappy. I was taught to accept that the cheese will move and that I'll have to get used to scavenging for and chasing cheese, because that's the way things are. Or, I could become 'a mouse like no other' who doesn't really need much cheese for some reason."

"I see," said Jim. "Did they explain why some people can do without cheese?"

"Um, not really. At least I don't think so. I mean, I'm not sure I was convinced that I could be the kind of mouse who'd be happy with little or no cheese."

Denis spoke up again. "That's good. That's called intro-spection and self-awareness. It's good to be honest with yourself about your feelings, especially when it comes to important subjects like cheese."

"Agreed," said Jim. "Did they happen to tell you *what cheese is* in those books? What I mean is, did they *define* cheese for you?"

"Define cheese?" Earl asked. "No, they didn't define cheese. Cheese is, well, cheese. What else could cheese be, if not cheese?"

"Oh, cheese is much more than cheese. Cheese, it seems to me, is a metaphor, Earl. But it's not a metaphor for just one thing. In other words, there are many types of cheese.

"I think, in general, those books meant to define cheese as something that could be used as a means of currency. It seems they substitute cheese for what people call *money*. Maybe it was meant to represent a job, or 'success,' too, but that's about all it seemed to embody when I read those books. What do you think?"

"Yeah," said Earl, in agreement. "I think I took it pretty much the same way."

"What if I told you there was a lot more to cheese than just something you could pile up, eat, and exchange?" asked Jim. "What would you say to that?"

"I guess I would say that I was surprised," said Earl. "I guess I'd say I have more to learn."

"Excellent," offered Brian.

"Yes, excellent," continued Bob. "Cheese takes many shapes, textures, sizes, flavors, aromas and consistencies. The types of cheeses the maze has to offer are virtually limitless. In fact, cheese is only limited by your creative imagination. You can make any cheese your heart desires."

"M . . . mmm . . . muh . . . make cheese?" Earl stammered. "No mouse has *ever made* cheese!" he insisted, now getting a bit irritated for the first time. "Mice *chase* cheese. They *find* cheese. They *gather* cheese. They *consume* cheese. But, they *don't make* cheese! The cheese is made *outside* the maze."

"There *is* no *outside* the maze," Denis reminded the young mouse.

"I don't understand," Earl admitted, sounding dejected. "I'm lost again. Please do something to explain. This is revolutionary for me. I've never heard any of this before."

"That's why you're here," began Bob. "You're here to gain awareness. Maybe it *is* a 'revolt' of sorts. It's a revolt against the old you. This philosophy represents a sweeping rejection of your old way of thinking and a comprehensive awakening of your immense potential.

"You have embarked upon a quest for heightened awareness. That process encompasses a heightened awareness of yourself, the maze within you, and the maze you live within. Hopefully, we can help you arrive at a practical and applicable understanding of the parallel maze as well."

"Here we go with this parallel maze thing again!" blurted Earl. "What are you talking about?" he asked, now looking totally exasperated.

"There is a parallel maze where self-reliant mice make their own cheese—any cheese—and as much cheese as they want. The parallel maze is the maze of freedom and happiness. It's a place where you can produce and enjoy as much cheese as you wish; and you can never take more than your share."

"Never take more than your share?" Earl questioned. "How is that possible? Mustn't we be cautious not to take too much, so that there is enough cheese to ensure that every mouse gets a little bit?"

"It's possible because the source is limitless," said Bob. "There is an ancient mouse philosophy that states: The mouse took abundance from abundance, and still . . . abundance remained."

This called for another low-toned, smooth whistle from Jim's steady lips. "Heavy," Jim said. "And so true," he added.

"Okay boys, let's slow down and back up for a second. This is all brand new to Earl," Bob said. "We must remember that we've been studying these *laws*, and how they work, for decades. He's only been at it for an hour or so.

"Earl, let's talk about what cheese really is," Bob continued.

"Okay," said Earl. "I've gotta hear this."

"Cheese is everything," Bob began. "Without cheese,

there's nothing, just like the nothing that exists outside the maze. There is nothing attractive nor redemptive about having nothing or existing in nothingness.

"Cheese is anything you wish it to be in your conscious mind. If you focus on the cheese you want for long enough, it will be adopted by the subconscious mind as it eventually crosses the psychic barrier. It will then manifest in reality through a process we call *transmutation*. Your body's actions will follow the paradigm and you will make your own cheese. Ultimately, it is your thinking that produces the tangible results you desire in the real world. It's a powerful system.

"In addition, through the sensory apparatus of your superconscious mind and the broadcasting mechanism of your paradigmatic mind, you will invite, attract, and acquire the specific resources and knowledge necessary to make all the cheeses you wish for. We call this process the *law of attraction*. Let me show you with the mind mouse," he said. Bob turned to the wall and sketched a few modifications so that Earl could see exactly what he meant. Here's what Earl saw:

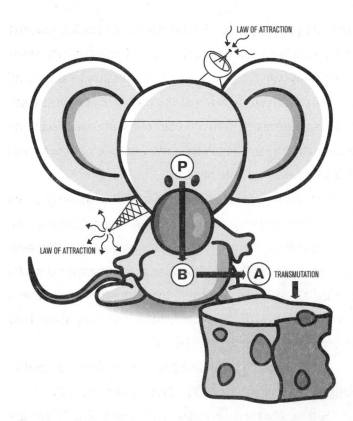

"I can see what you're all getting at," said Earl, "but this is so different from how I've been accustomed to thinking. This cheese concept is a little abstract, I must admit. Can you give me some concrete examples of cheese? I think that would be really helpful. Cheese seemed so limited and unappealing after I read the other books. I wasn't even sure if cheese was something I wanted any more. I certainly wasn't sure that I'd be happy chasing it all over the maze while being at the mercy of someone else's whims. The idea that an outsider had the power to decide where the cheese would be and how much cheese I was *allowed* never sat well with me."

"Let me handle this one," Jim said confidently, as he stood. "Cheese is the stuff of life," he began. "Cheese usually acts like a magnifying lens. If you give lots of cheese to a good mouse, he tends to become a great mouse. If a mouse is a jerk, and acquires a lot of cheese, he becomes a bigger jerk. But, I don't think we have to worry about that in your case. Right, Earl?"

"That's right, Sir, we don't have to worry about that in my case. I am a good mouse," Earl replied, humbly.

"Bravo. Then I'll proceed," continued Jim. "Here are some examples of the cheeses you can make in order to live *the good life*:

"There is professional success cheese and money cheese. There's high-income cheese and savings for retirement cheese. There is good health cheese and happiness cheese. There's rent and mortgage and health insurance premium cheese. There's listening to good music cheese and dancing cheese. There's going to a party cheese and there's taking a nice nap on a Saturday afternoon cheese. There's playing a musical instrument cheese. There is hugs cheese and kisses cheese. There's making love cheese and holding hands cheese. There's writing poetry cheese and reading a great thriller cheese. There's watching movies with your family cheese and family dinners on Sunday cheese. There's also material object cheese. This kind of cheese may take the form of car cheese, house cheese, fine art cheese, diamond ring cheese, ruby necklace cheese, Swiss wristwatch cheese, pleasure boat cheese, golf clubs cheese, fine clothing cheese, new shoes cheese, or any other kind of stuff you want cheese. There is also charity and generosity and sharing cheese. You'll find these cheeses in the 'giving' section of your cheese factory. This area of your personal manufacturing plant also includes philanthropy cheese. Then there is education and tuition cheese. There's also travel and adventure cheese. There's business cheese and vacation cheese. There's solitude cheese and quiet cheese as well as friendship cheese and celebration cheese. There's exercise cheese. This group of cheeses includes running cheese and walking cheese and hiking cheese and skiing cheese and golfing cheese and fishing cheese and yoga cheese and tennis cheese and all kinds of fun, healthy cheeses. There's meditation cheese and mindfulness cheese and gratitude cheese. There's peaceful cheese. There's joyful cheese. There's anything you can possibly imagine cheese! And they're all inside of you. They're all inside of your fabulous mind, right this second. It's your choice whether you wish to bring them out and give form to them in the physical realm. If you choose to do so it can really happen. The decision is yours, and yours alone, Earl."

Then Jim paused. He became very still. He became as quiet as a church mouse. Everyone's imaginations were taking them to wonderful places. They saw themselves doing all the exciting things life had to offer. They imagined sharing these experiences with the mice they loved.

After several moments, Jim broke his silence and said, "Earl, the real question to ask is not, 'how much cheese,' or 'what kind of cheese will I get in the parallel maze?' The real question to ask is 'who will I have to become to get to the parallel maze?' I think you should set a goal to have all that cheese because of the mouse you'll have to become in order to *earn* that much cheese."

Earl thought deeply about everything Jim had just said. He was swept away in profound reflection. He meditated deeply for several minutes. Opening his eyes slowly, Earl said, "I've never thought about cheese this way before. Somehow, the other books gave me the impression that cheese stinks. But now I think I could really learn to like this kind of cheese. I want to become the kind of mouse who deserves all that cheese."

"That's good, Earl," said Denis. "Because cheese is neither good nor bad. Only the mice who possess the cheese can be good or bad."

"Yes, I see that now," said Earl. "I'd definitely like to taste some of the cheese that Jim described. It sounds absolutely delicious! How can I start making my cheese? I'd like to get started!" he exclaimed.

"Well the best way," said a distant sounding voice "would be to take a quantum leap."

Chapter 7

Quantum Leap

And then, seemingly out of the ether, appeared another well-groomed grey-haired mouse wearing spectacles.

"Ah, Price," said Napoleon, "so good to see you! We weren't sure if you were going to be able to make it."

Price went around the circle and shook paws with all those assembled, trading respectful pleasantries and greetings as he did.

"Oh yes, I've been here the entire time. I was just curled up in another dimension where you couldn't see me. But I've been listening intently to your robust conversation. It seems we have a very gifted pupil with us today."

There were vigorous nods of agreement amongst his colleagues. "Outstanding," he said. "It seems young Earl here would like to travel across the terror barrier and make his way to freedom and happiness. It seems he has had his fill of conformity and bondage, eh?"

Again, everyone concurred.

"Okay then, let's get right into it," Price said. "You see, Earl, there is a parallel maze right alongside us. You can't see the maze, but the maze is there. In fact, all of *us* are in the other maze right now. You can see us, but you can't see our maze. But make no mistake; you are *not* in the same maze as us."

"I don't understand," said Earl.

"I wouldn't expect you to, Earl," said Price. "Try to see that you are in a maze we call *conformity and bondage*. We are in a maze called *freedom and happiness*."

Bob, interrupted politely and said, "Here, take a look at this drawing; it may help you to visualize what Price is trying to say," as he began to sketch feverishly. "Remember," he said, "this is simply a diagrammatic representation. In reality each of the mazes go on and on forever, they have no true limits to their dimensions. The key is to see how they exist in parallel, right next to one another, separated only by the terror barrier." He stood back to reveal the following drawing:

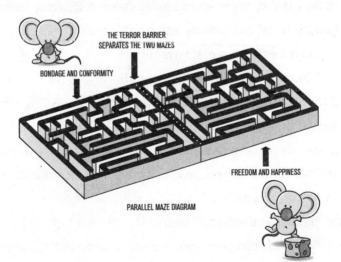

THE TERROR BARRIER
SEPARATES THE TWO MAZES

BONDAGE AND CONFORMITY

FREEDOM AND HAPPINESS

PARALLEL MAZE DIAGRAM

The reason we live here and you live there is because of the way you've been thinking. We don't think the way you do any more. We are free because we have all crossed through the terror barrier a long time ago. We took a quantum leap. It happens all at once. It happens in a moment. It only takes an instant. It's like an electron suddenly shifting orbits around the nucleus. It's effortless and happens in a flash. One moment you are at one level of vibration and the next moment you have been elevated to a much higher energy field. The process is instantaneous and based on a personal decision to make the leap. When it happens, it takes no time at all, but it does require one very special personal attribute."

"What attribute is that?" asked Earl.

"Courage," said Price, in a serious tone. "Courage is the essential trait that every mouse must possess if they wish to take the quantum leap across the terror barrier."

Jim chimed in, "Those are called *the facts.*"

"If you can muster the courage to first change your mind, you can then take that leap and change your life forever. You can be on the other side with us. You would exist at a higher state of being. You would be living at a more energized frequency. You can make, eat, have, enjoy, and share as much cheese as you like on the other side of the maze. The source is endless. You can have any kind of cheese and any amount of cheese you desire.

"Here, let me show you with a drawing," he said, as he politely motioned to Bob for the chalk. He erased what had been there before and took his time to draw a fairly elaborate diagram. It looked like this:

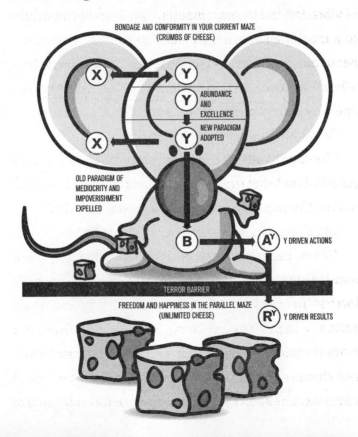

"Wow," said Earl. "That's awesome! My life would be perfect over there. I *really* want to live in the parallel maze. The maze of freedom and happiness. The maze of unlimited cheese!"

"Yes," said Price "you *do* want to live over here; but let me be absolutely clear . . . *no* maze is perfect. Even in the maze of freedom and happiness there are problems. There is always a *price to pay*. You still have to work extremely hard to make your cheese. Cheese-making isn't easy work. What you put in, you will get out. Remember the garden of the subconscious mind. As you sow, so shall you reap. That's *the law*.

"The parallel maze is not heaven on earth. It's still a maze with all its twists and turns, dark corridors, and blind passages. Even in the parallel maze there are sacrifices, responsibilities, difficulties, and disappointments. Some years, there may be a blight and the harvest may be lost. Other years, conditions may be ideal and the soil produces a bumper crop. Even in the parallel maze, mice get sick, mice get old, and mice die."

Jim interjected, "That's called *reality*." He said the last word with a slightly higher pitch and drew it out long and slow, to put extra emphasis on its importance.

"But it's still a hell of a lot better than the way you're living now," said, Bob. "The parallel maze is a place where you stand on your own two feet and forge your own destiny. You are limited only by your own magnificent imagination, ambition, and appetite for cheese."

"The parallel maze is where the harsh fluorescent light of the conformity maze is replaced with the reassuring blue sky of freedom and self-determination," interjected Brian.

"Yes," continued Bob. "That's true. It's the maze of abundance. It holds abundance of all kinds. But, in order to make the leap, you must decide that you are willing to *make your own damn cheese!*" said Bob, emphatically. He was almost shouting. He was so excited he was practically sparkling with energy. All the mice were exhilarated by his tremendous enthusiasm.

"That's exactly what I need to do," said Earl, as his eyes became wide and flooded with desire. "I need to make my own damn cheese!"

"That's the attitude!" exclaimed Brian.

"*Attitude*? That's a curious word. What role does attitude play in all of this?" asked Earl.

"Earl, that would be like asking 'what role does milk play in cheese?' or 'what role do the walls play in the maze?' It's not everything, Earl, but it's nearly everything. When it comes to the subjects of success, happiness, and freedom, attitude is essentially everything," said Denis emphatically.

Chapter 8

Blue Sky Thinking

"**E**arl," Denis continued, "a moment ago, Brian mentioned the blue sky of freedom."

"Yes, I remember," said Earl. "That sounds beautiful."

"Yes, indeed it does. Have you ever heard of blue sky *thinking*?"

"No, I haven't," responded Earl. "I must admit, that's a new term for me as well."

"Would you like to explain it to him, Brian?" asked Denis.

"I'd be happy to," Brian said as he took the chalk and headed to the wall to draw.

"We are coming near the close of all this, Earl. You're probably relieved to hear that."

"A bit, I must admit," answered Earl. "But not because I'm not enjoying myself; I am. It feels like I've learned more today than I've learned in my entire life. It's just that I want to get to work building my factory and making my cheese."

"I understand," said Brian. "You'll have plenty of time for that. But first, let me share a key piece of the puzzle that makes it all work. This will allow the entire process to come together and function in a meaningful and productive way: you must begin to set goals."

"Goals?" repeated Earl, with a questioning tone.

"Yes, Earl, goals," said Brian. "You must ask yourself, what would my world look like if it were perfect in every conceivable way? Which cheeses would I make? How much cheese would I have? Where would I live and make my cheese? With whom would I spend my time and share my cheese? How would I behave? How would I dress? In a perfect maze, how would everything be, assuming it wouldn't harm any other mouse in any way?

"This is what we call *blue sky* thinking, Earl. It's very important that you begin to adopt this kind of thinking in your life, or nothing will ever change."

Jim interrupted, "Nothing will change until you change, Earl. And when you change, everything will change for you."

"I understand," said Earl. "And I'm ready to change. How do I begin?"

"You begin by setting goals," said Brian. "That means deciding *exactly* what you want and writing it down. Take a piece of chalk and write on the wall. Make a list of everything your heart desires. Don't ask for what you think you *can* have, or what you think you *can* achieve. Ask for what you *really want*. That's a different thing altogether. That's blue sky thinking. But, let me warn you—it can be really scary. You'll probably find that your current paradigm will be convinced that you don't really deserve everything you really want. Your paradigm will tell you that you're not worthy of that kind of success. The paradigm always seems to be set to make us feel much smaller than we really are."

"Yes," said Earl. "I know what you mean. Even when I was digging my tunnel, I would often think to myself, *Who do you think you are that you deserve better than what this maze has to offer? If it was good enough for your mother and father, your sisters and your brothers, and all of your friends, what makes you think that it's not good enough for you?*"

"Exactly," said Brian. "But you do deserve more. Every mouse does. But it begins with the thinking in your conscious mind. This is where the goals get set. One must focus on these goals—every day. You must think about them and write them down, over and over, for a long time. You must get emotionally involved with them. Then, and only then, if you have the *courage* to stick with your blue sky thinking will these new goals cross the psychic barrier and be adopted as the new paradigm. When this occurs, your behavior will change and so will your results. Look here," he said, as he began to draw:

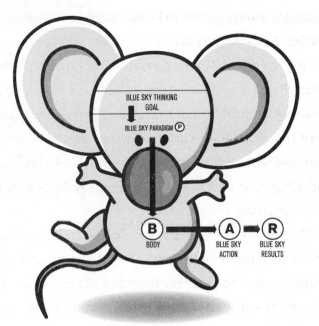

"It's beautiful," said Earl. "It's really beautiful."

"It is," answered Brian. "But, it's much more challenging than it looks."

"I can image it is," said Earl. "But, at least now I know how it really works."

"That's right," said Brian. "That's the awareness one must possess in order to make a deliberate and conscious

quantum leap to living the good life. Without that understanding, the chances are very slim that things will ever
change for the better. Some mice do stumble their way
into the good life through dumb luck or a crack in the
maze, but very few. That's not an approach we suggest
you take. You can do better than that."

Chapter 9

The Great Revelation

"There's something else I'd like to share with you, Earl. Would that be okay?" asked Bob.

"Of course," said Earl. "What is it?"

"Alright," said Bob. "Earl, why don't you take a seat for this. I think it would be better if you were sitting down."

"Okay," said Earl, as he made himself comfortable on the floor alongside Jim, Brian, Denis, Price, and Napoleon.

"Earl," Bob continued, "do you remember when you first met Napoleon and he said he wanted to introduce you to yourself?"

"Sure I do," said Earl, with a big smile. "And he has! I know so much more about who I am now than I did a few hours ago. I know what my mind looks like, and much more about how it functions. I understand now how I can control my mind to design my blue sky parallel maze of freedom and happiness. I understand the mind-body connection and how my thoughts will drive my actions. I understand how my actions will function to build my new maze. I understand that it takes courage to introduce new goals in order to break through the psychic barrier and reprogram my paradigm. I also recognize that it takes courage to take action and break through the terror barrier so that I can enjoy freedom and happiness. I know I can make my own cheese. I feel like I know myself better than I ever have before."

"That's wonderful," said Bob, as the others nodded in unanimous agreement. "But there's something else. There is something very *big* you must understand about yourself for this to truly make sense and be put into effect."

"What's that, Bob? What is it that I need to know?" asked Earl, sounding concerned.

"It's something the other books didn't share. They kept an important secret from you. They withheld a vitally important truth, Earl."

"Okay, okay," said Earl, starting to sound a bit impatient again. "What is this great truth that I must know? What is this secret?"

"The truth is, Earl, you're not a mouse," said Bob, with a tone of seriousness he hadn't used previously.

"Not a mouse?" responded Earl, in utter disbelief. "Don't be ridiculous. If I'm not a mouse, Bob, then what am I?"

"You're a *man*, Earl. You are *not* a mouse. You're a human being. And, you're not a 'little person' either. You're a full-grown, real life, normal-sized, man."

The blood suddenly drained out of Earl's brain and face without warning. He went as white as a bed sheet. His vision went black. He was unconscious. This is why Bob had asked him to sit down. Bob had seen this kind of reaction before.

The next thing Earl knew, Jim was gently tapping his cheek, saying, "Earl, are you alright? Come on lad, you're alright. Wake up. Everything is going to be fine."

Earl looked around and he saw six men sitting around him in a beautifully appointed conference room. As he looked down at his own hands, he could plainly see that they were the hands of a person, not a mouse. "Of course," he said to himself, "now it's all so clear."

Earl smiled and said, "That's why the other books never really made sense to me. They were far too simplistic. They were like children's stories. How could the life of a human being be compared to that of a mouse? It's not possible."

"That's right," said Jim. "You see, Earl, what makes you so exceptional, so extraordinary, is your mind. It's not the mind of a mouse; it's the mind of a human being. You have higher mental faculties, like imagination, will, perception, reason, memory, and intuition. You were not put here to scurry around sniffing about for crumbs of cheese. You were put here to think *BIG*. You were put here to function as a co-creator of the world you live in, not as a spectator. Certainly, you were never meant to be a victim or the subject of some overly simplistic laboratory experiment sniffing out meaningless morsels of cheese.

"You are not like a mouse who can only follow the scent of the cheese. You are not like any other animal. You are not like a goose who can only fly south in the winter. You are a self-actualized person. You possess the unbridled power of *free will*. You have the power to choose *precisely* how you want to live. You are not like a goose at all. You can choose to go north or east or west, or any way you wish. You can also decide to change direction any time you like. You have had the extraordinary good fortune to be born the highest form of life in the universe. You can use your brilliant mind to set goals and fall in love with them. You can create sophisticated plans and be the architect of all your hopes and dreams. You can build any lifestyle you wish to enjoy, all beginning with an idea. Your thoughts are things. The choice is yours. You have the ability to think any way you want to think, regardless of your current circumstances. You can set any goals you desire. You can pursue whatever it is you truly want from life. This truth is the greatest truth there is. It's also the greatest power we human beings have been blessed with."

Earl was elated. Then and there he decided that his tunnel digging days were over, and his building days were just beginning. There was no need to escape, only to change, starting with his thinking. In an instant, he took the leap. He made up his mind to change, and everything began to change for him. The great revelation freed him from the maze of bondage and conformity. At once, he was transported to a new world of opportunity, freedom and happiness.

He made his own "cheese," and lots of it. He enjoyed it himself and shared it generously with others. He put other people to work and encouraged them to be the best they could be. Earl never felt, behaved, or looked like a mouse again. He stopped seeing himself as a mouse. He killed the mouse inside of him that day and he let the man be born. He stopped chasing happiness and started attracting it to himself by the person he had become.

He became self-reliant and he also demonstrated self-determination in all of his thoughts and deeds. He was no longer small or unimportant. He became *a man like no other*. The world was not a prison for Earl; it was a cornucopia of limitless possibility and achievement.

Rather than run from his life, he embraced and cherished every moment of it. He shared his story, and his knowledge, with anyone who had the desire to listen. And he lived happily ever after under the blue skies of the parallel maze.

The End

About the Author

John A. Chuback, MD, FACS, is an accomplished physician, surgeon, inventor, author, philanthropist, businessman and educator. He is Board Certified in General Surgery and Cardiovascular Surgery. He received his Medical Degree from Rutgers University and enjoys a robust private practice in Paramus, New Jersey. Dr. Chuback is also a successful entrepreneur. Besides being Chief Medical Officer at Chuback Medical Group, he is also CEO at Chuback Education, LLC. This dynamic company offers programs on personal development and the power of individual achievement. The focus at Chuback Education is creating awareness of the massive potential of the human mind. Dr. Chuback also built *BiosupportMD.com*, a nutraceutical company whose goal is to use ingredients found in nature to help people live healthier and better lives. He is the recipient of numerous professional awards and honors.

To learn more about John Chuback and available resources such as books, audio programs, speaking engagements, and upcoming seminars, please visit *chubackeducation.com*.